20 FUN FACTS ABOUT NATIVE AMERICAN WOMEN

By Caitie McAneney

Gareth Stevens
PUBLISHING

Please visit our website, www.garethstevens.com. For a free color catalog of all our high-quality books, call toll free 1-800-542-2595 or fax 1-877-542-2596.

Library of Congress Cataloging-in-Publication Data

McAneney, Caitie.
  20 fun facts about Native American women / Caitie McAneney.
    pages cm — (Fun Fact File: Women in History.)
  Includes bibliographical references and index.
  ISBN 978-1-4824-2808-7 (pbk.)
  ISBN 978-1-4824-2809-4 (6 pack)
  ISBN 978-1-4824-2810-0 (library binding)
  1. Indian women—Biography—Juvenile literature. I. Title.

  E98.W8M33 2015
  305.48'897—dc23

                                    2015006055

First Edition

Published in 2016 by
Gareth Stevens Publishing
111 East 14th Street, Suite 349
New York, NY 10003

Copyright © 2016 Gareth Stevens Publishing

Designer: Samantha DeMartin
Editor: Kristen Rajczak

Photo credits: Cover, p. 1 Culture Club/Hulton Archive/Getty Images; p. 5 Jerome Pollos/Getty Images News/ Getty Images; pp. 6, 29 Marilyn Angel Wynn/Nativestock/Getty Images; p. 7 Archive Photos/Archive Photos/ Getty Images; p. 8 courtesy of Library of Congress; p. 9 Harvey Meston/Archive Photos/Getty Images; p. 9 (Chilkat robe) Mary Ebbetts Hunt/Wikimedia Commons; p. 10 (Iroquois) Frank A. Rinehart/Wikimedia Commons; p. 10 (Hopi) Charles C. Pierce/Wikimedia Commons; p. 10 (Inuit) Topical Press Agency/Hulton Archive/Getty Images; p. 10 (Cherokee) Popperfoto/Popperfoto/Getty Images ,pp. 11, 15, 18 Hulton Archive/ Hulton Archive/Getty Images; pp. 10 (Tlingit), 12 Buyenlarge/Archive Photos/Getty Images; p. 13 Ted Russell/ The LIFE Picture Collection/Getty Images; p. 14 Google Cultural Institute/Wikimedia Commons; p. 16 MPI/ Archive Photos/Getty Images; p. 17 Kean Collection/Archive Photos/Getty Images; p. 19 otterlove/Creative Commons/Flickr.com; p. 20 Leemage/Universal Images Group/Getty Images; p. 21 Charles Marion Russell/ Wikimedia Commons; p. 22 Joelwnelson/Wikimedia Commons; p. 23 courtesy of Arizona State University; p. 24 PETER PARKS/AFP/Getty Images; p. 25 Darren McCollester/Hulton Archive/Getty Images; p. 26 PAUL J. RICHARDS/AFP/Getty Images.

Printed in the United States of America

CPSIA compliance information: Batch #CS15GS: For further information contact Gareth Stevens, New York, New York at 1-800-542-2595.

Contents

Words in the glossary appear in **bold** type the first time they are used in the text.

Powerful Women

Throughout history, Native American women have proved their strength and power. They played important **roles** in their tribes. While you might think they were mostly homemakers, their jobs and skills went far beyond that!

A woman's role depended on her tribe. In many tribes, women were honored for their talents. They did hard work, took care of their families, and could even be leaders of their **clan**! Some Native American women have made history for their accomplishments as brave leaders and groundbreakers.

Most Native American women don't live like they used to. However, they keep their culture, or way of life, alive by practicing their **traditions**.

5

Traditional Roles

Native American women built their own homes.

Women of the Powhatan tribe were in charge of building houses called *yehakins*. They gathered saplings, or young trees, to make the frame and covered them in mats and bark. They also collected firewood for their new home.

This dwelling with an arched roof was built to look like a Powhatan yehakin.

Women of the Great Plains went on buffalo hunts.

As the men of the tribe hunted and killed buffalo for food and clothing, the women helped set up tepees and tear apart the meat of the buffalo. They sometimes carried the meat back to their village, too.

Great Plains tribes relied on buffalo for food, clothes, shelter, and tools.

Not all medicine men were men. Some tribes had medicine women!

Women were often considered healers in their tribe. They knew traditional ways of healing, which were passed down. Women collected plants to make medicines. They especially helped with childbirth.

In traditional Native American culture, women were believed to have special healing powers.

Chilkat robe

Navajo women have been making traditional pottery for hundreds of years.

FACT 4

Women were often the keepers of culture in their tribe.

Women often made their tribe's food, clothing, and art, and passed down songs and traditions to their children. In the Chilkat tribe of the Pacific Northwest, women have made beautiful robes for centuries. This helps keep their culture alive.

Traditional Women's Clothing

Tribes and Their Dress

Iroquois women wore dresses made of deerskin decorated with beads and belts. They wore beautiful and colorful headbands.

Hopi women dressed for warm weather. They wore thin knee-length dresses with one shoulder. They wore moccasins made of deerskin.

Tlingit women dressed for both the warm and cold weather of the Pacific Northwest Coast. They wore skirts made of bark and deerskin. For special occasions, they wore decorative clothing and colorful Chilkat blankets.

Inuit women wore clothing made of animal skin and fur to stay warm in their cold surroundings. They wore coats with hoods big enough to hold their babies. They wore high boots made of animal skin and fur.

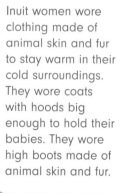

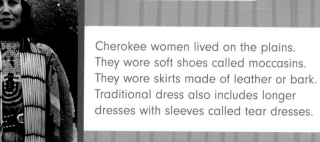

Cherokee women lived on the plains. They wore soft shoes called moccasins. They wore skirts made of leather or bark. Traditional dress also includes longer dresses with sleeves called tear dresses.

Leadership and Power

Women ruled over the family in many tribes.

Matrilineal tribes, such as the Iroquois, were those that

traced their family line through the mother's family. In addition, when a Hopi man and woman were married, they went to live with the woman's family.

Women weren't often tribe leaders, but they were wholly in charge of their home.

In matrilineal tribes, women owned all the property.

In the Hopi culture, women owned all goods, crops, land, and homes. Women **inherited** property from their family. If a marriage ended, the woman kept all property, and the man had to leave the home with nothing.

The Tlingit tribe of the Pacific Northwest and the Iroquois nation of the Northeast were both matrilineal peoples.

In some tribes, women were able to appoint their leaders.

American women didn't gain voting rights until 1920. However, Iroquois women had a voice in tribal government for hundreds of years. Iroquois women had the power to appoint tribal leaders and make sure they did their job.

The oldest women in a clan, or family, had the most power to appoint leaders.

FACT 8

The real Pocahontas was kidnapped by English settlers.

The movie *Pocahontas* shows a young Native American woman falling in love with a settler, John Smith. In real life, Pocahontas was kidnapped by the English and forced to take on their ways. She married Englishman John Rolfe, went to England, and died young.

Pocahontas was the daughter of Chief Powhatan. The Powhatan tribe and English settlers often didn't get along during the early years of English settlement in Virginia.

14

Savannah, Georgia, might not have been founded without the help of a Creek woman.

In 1717, Mary Musgrove, a Native American of the Creek tribe, married an English trader and opened a trading post in Georgia. She helped the English and the Yamacraw tribe understand each other so Georgia's settlement could be peaceful.

Mary Musgrove was a successful interpreter and businesswoman.

Sacagawea was a symbol of peace to Native American tribes who had yet to meet any Europeans.

Sacagawea was a member of the Shoshone tribe. In 1805, she joined explorers Lewis and Clark on their journey to the Pacific Coast. She interpreted for them and showed the tribes they met the group was friendly.

Sacagawea made the whole trip from North Dakota to the Pacific Ocean carrying her baby son.

During the American Revolution, many Native American women were members of tribes that didn't take sides during the war.

FACT 11

One Native American woman was a spy during the American Revolution.

Molly Brant was the daughter of a Mohawk sachem, or chief, and lived with an important English colonist. She became a famous **loyalist** who secretly passed knowledge to the British!

FACT 12

European explorers and settlers in Pennsylvania learned to pay their respects to Queen Aliquippa—including George Washington!

Aliquippa was the leader of a Seneca tribe in the 1700s. Her tribe lived near present-day Pittsburgh, Pennsylvania. She was an important supporter of the British during the French and Indian War.

Aliquippa and George Washington met more than once when he was a young man leading British troops.

Queen Cockacoeske became chief of the Pamunkey tribe in Virginia upon her husband's death.

In 1677, Cockacoeske signed the Treaty of Middle Plantation, which swore loyalty to the British. The British sent her queen's clothing as a gift and forced tribes to unite under her power. Some wouldn't, however.

Cockacoeske
(1640-1686)

Queen Cockacoeske ruled the Pamunkey until she died in 1686.

FACT 14

Some Apache women fought just as fiercely as the men in their tribe.

Lozen was an Apache warrior and **shaman** who fought alongside her brother, an Apache chief, in many battles against the American and Mexican armies during the late 1800s. One of Lozen's companions was Dahteste, an Apache woman who fought in many **raids.**

Lozen was believed to have powers that helped her defeat her enemies in battle. She fought alongside famous Apache warrior Geronimo, too.

The Cheyenne people say that Buffalo Calf Road Woman may have been the one to knock Lieutenant Colonel Custer off his horse before he died in the Battle of the Little Bighorn.

FACT 15

Buffalo Calf Road Woman saved her brother, a chief, during battle.

In 1876, Chief Comes in Sight was leading his Cheyenne tribe against the US Army in the Battle of the Rosebud. His horse was shot and he was hurt, but his sister Buffalo Calf Road Woman saved him. She also fought in the Battle of the Little Bighorn.

Famous Firsts

FACT 16

The first Native American woman to become a doctor founded a hospital on her home reservation.

Susan La Flesche Picotte was born on the Omaha Reservation in Nebraska in 1865. After attending the Women's Medical College of Pennsylvania, she returned to the reservation as a doctor and founded a hospital there in 1913.

Today, the Dr. Susan La Flesche Picotte Memorial Hospital has a museum in memory of its founder.

In 2014, the first Native American woman to serve as a US federal judge was appointed.

Diane Humetewa, a Hopi woman, served as a lawyer and judge for the Hopi tribe. She was also a US **attorney** in Arizona from 2007 to 2009.

As a federal judge, Humetewa can be a voice for the many Native American people living in Arizona.

Dawn Kelly Allen was one of the first women inducted, or accepted, into the American Indian Athletic Hall of Fame.

Dawn Kelly Allen was born in 1955 in Oklahoma. She belonged to the Quapaw, Cherokee, and Euchee tribes. She was a women's tennis champion in the National North American Indian Tennis Championships for most years from 1976 to 1991.

Mary Killman is another successful Native American athlete. She was on the US synchronized swimming team in the 2012 Olympics!

Ryneldi Becenti was the first Native American to play in the Women's National Basketball Association (WNBA).

Born in Arizona in 1971, Becenti grew up on a Navajo reservation. She played basketball at Arizona State University. As part of the US team, she won a bronze medal at the World University Games in 1993.

Winona LaDuke was the first Native American woman to run for US vice president.

25

Wilma Mankiller was the first female principal chief of the Cherokee Nation.

Wilma Mankiller was born into the Cherokee tribe in Oklahoma in 1945. Mankiller went to college and joined the American Indian **activist** movement. She served as the Cherokee principal chief from 1985 to 1995. She worked to improve Cherokee schools, government, and health care.

In 1998, Mankiller was honored with the Presidential Medal of Freedom, one of the highest honors given in the United States.

Keeping History Alive

Native American women keep their history alive today in many ways.

Keeping Languages Alive

Many tribes were forced to give up their language and learn English. Women like Natalie Diaz, coordinator of the Fort Mojave Language Recovery Program, work to understand native languages and record them.

Making Traditional Artwork

Women of the Pueblo tribes continue to make beautiful pottery, keeping their tribes' stories and beliefs alive in the clay.

Performing Traditional Dances

Most tribes valued traditional songs and dances for celebrations. Today, women still learn and perform these dances. Women of the Nanticoke tribe perform dances that show the importance of women as life givers, homemakers, and voices in the community.

Embracing Education

The number of Native American women going to college is increasing even faster than Native American men. These women can use their education to improve schools and daily life on reservations and call attention to the rich culture and history of their people.

Strong Women, Strong History

Life for Native American women has never been easy. They had to work hard to take care of their tribe. They survived many wars between tribes and with Europeans. They were forced from their homelands onto reservations. Even today, many Native American women suffer from lack of schooling and money.

The success of Native American women is often overlooked. It's important to celebrate the great things they have accomplished. These strong women helped build cultures and keep them alive today.

Wearing traditional clothing is one way Native American women honor their culture.

activist: one who acts strongly in support of or against an issue or cause

attorney: someone who works for others in a court of law

clan: a group of related families

inherit: to get by legal right after a person's death

interpreter: someone who can tell the meaning of another language

loyalist: someone who was loyal to the British during the American Revolution

medicine: a drug taken to make a sick person well

raid: a sudden attack

reservation: land set aside by the US government for Native Americans

role: the part a person plays

shaman: a person believed to be connected to the spirit world and to have special powers

tradition: a long-practiced custom

For More Information

Books

Bruchac, James. *The Girl Who Helped Thunder and Other Native American Folktales.* New York, NY: Sterling Publishing Co., 2008.

Colich, Abby. *Wilma Mankiller.* North Mankato: MN: Capstone Press, 2015.

Norwich, Grace. *I Am Sacagawea.* New York, NY: Scholastic Inc., 2012.

Websites

Native American: Clothing
www.ducksters.com/history/native_american_clothing.php
Learn more about Native American clothing, including how it's made and how it has changed.

Native Americans in Olden Times: For Kids
nativeamericans.mrdonn.org/index.html
Explore facts about many Native American tribes, including how and where they lived.

Publisher's note to educators and parents: Our editors have carefully reviewed these websites to ensure that they are suitable for students. Many websites change frequently, however, and we cannot guarantee that a site's future contents will continue to meet our high standards of quality and educational value. Be advised that students should be closely supervised whenever they access the Internet.